MW01278548

A Woman in Pieces Crossed a Sea

A Woman in Pieces Crossed a Sea

Denise Bergman

A Woman in Pieces Crossed a Sea
© 2014 by Denise Bergman.
Printed in the United States of America.

No part of this book may be performed, recorded, or otherwise transmitted without the written consent of the author and the permission of the publisher. However, portions of the poems may be cited for book reviews without gaining such consent.

First print edition: June, 2014
ISBN 978-0-9910742-2-8
West End Press | P.O. Box 27334 | Albuquerque, NM 87125

Front cover photographs: Library of Congress (headless statue), National Park Service (face)
Author photograph, rear cover: Janice Danielson
Typography and design: Lila Sanchez

For book information, see our website at www.westendpress.org

For Gerry & Artis

In 1886 the Statue of Liberty was unveiled in New York City's harbor.

The statue was a gift from the French people to the United States to celebrate both US independence and the Union's victory in the Civil War.

The sculptor was Frederic Auguste Bartholdi.

Fifteen storeys tall, the sculpture was fabricated in Colmar, France, then disassembled into 350 pieces and shipped to Bedloe's Island, its permanent home.

For one long year the statue remained in 214 crates.

The reassembled woman is constructed of thin sheets of copper repoussé riveted to a skeletal steel armature.

A Woman in Pieces Crossed a Sea

TABLE OF CONTENTS

HEY LADY

Hey lady! You
or her, you turn your head

Hey
lady lady lady—
who? The tight-lipped goddess

or one of you

running your husband's lunchbox
down the Brooklyn docks

hello—hey—
wait

Hey lady!
Not a whisper, this catcall.

Give us
what you promised, or give us

an honest truth

c'mere and look me
in the eye.

Colmar, France

MOTHER

Mother, sit down, sit—
you made
me
and I'll

make
your likeness.
Just think

you'll open the harbor,
my name
at your feet.

THE SCULPTOR AND HIS MOTHER

He knows no shackles
or shackles' welt,
no gash in a child's bosom, her mother
torn away.
He hasn't seen
this history's
bone-exposed bone.

But an artist can imagine,
sketch and build.
He thinks: each baby's first breath
is a breath.
Let mother be the look
he's looking for.

Where to start—

where did he start
and when did he know to break her
into parts,
when did he decide

stages of her reconstruction.

Germ of a colossal notion
the Sphinx, Rhodes.
A gist, handful, cake of ore,
commission secure,
do it big.
Mother on a stool beside the easel
turns three-quarters around.
Almond eyes, lids, chin—he sketches
top to bottom,
head to broken-shackle feet.

HEAD

Below a doubting brow, frowning eyes
open.

Windows in her diadem. Eyes are not enough
and no visible tearducts.

A triangle widow's peak.
Two wound-up
pincurls on her temples. At her nape
uncombed plaits.

Her lower lip pouts.
Top to bottom: brow, frown, pout,
chin.

An articulated chin means something,
high cheekbones

signify "class." On any face
uplifted

eyes perpetually look down.

EYES

Bartholdi Bartholdi
if this is your mother, shape her pupils, let her see.
Wide straight-ahead eyes are fine but
in the cerulean harbor
under a knotted net of pinhole suns

to be nearsighted will be nothing.
Farsighted, so what.
She'll trip on her own broken chain.

HER LIPS HE CARVES

Her lips he carves a snap-closed purse.
In a year we'll hear cold
coins jangling behind her teeth,
pennies, nickels, dimes, a lira, a sou.
Change, spare change
her lips will still lock in silence—

but now he squeezes clay wads
the size of spitballs.

BIG IS FAR BETTER

Colossal means his name will be shouted
Rhodes to Rome to Red Hook

alleys and dock to dock.
Set in hot type
in newsprint, on posters pasted to brick walls.

He mongers size
like a fishwife at the close of day

until *finally*, permission granted,
payment assured, go ahead.
Supplies, studio space, diagrams and sketches,
tea with his mother.
He swells in size
and in her eyes he swells in size,
his gateway is opening.

But why is big better, why does a loud
shout grab attention, squelch
the whisper.

Why assume small is timid and meek.

Why is big better yet a tall, wide,
strong-willed woman and her attributes
if you don't ignore, you deride.
Who, then, is this exception

and why

will she be better
big.

WHO HACKED THE SHACKLES OPEN

Who hacked them open
and did he note
the exact moment the mallet
first fell and the chisel
nicked the metal.
With chalk
did he mark location
or, experienced, did he eyeball
the spot where concept
grips an iron ring.
A precise cut or rough edges.
Spur of the moment
or redrawn draft to draft
an unreconfigured
sketch in ink from the start.
Who hacked them
and left the pieces, unremoved, in place.
Who said: breaking in half
will lighten a load.

THREE STAGES OF ENLARGEMENT
WITH 9000 MEASUREMENTS

What grows, suffers size.

Bartholdi measured proportions
time and time and time again

each metric jotting a skip and a jump
to the next
forged enlargement.

Suffer the size.
Liberty and metal expand at different rates,
surface and tension
mismatch.

What grows.
The sculptor measured his concept,
the concept measured up.
Proportions not too
disproportionate.
Hands, for example, as they should be,
wrist to fingertip
the length of a human face.
And if he opened the statue's arms she'd touch
the east/west
corners of Leonardo's circle.

AIR IS BALLAST

Air, fundamental
to any proper list of materials.
Air: her brain, her veins.
The varicose weight of her feet,
a frugal substitute for sand,
the original sway-prevention ballast plan.
Imagine sand
poured into permanent
confinement
to keep her skin a tethered
inflated balloon, no,

a hollow entitlement,
stability.

CRUCIBLE

Ironic,
iron pulled from the heat of earth
remelted
in a crucible that is iron too.
Ironic
like silt from a riverbottom
building the bank.
Like liberty and longing, or heartache
overtaking a heart.
Ironic, like trial
and trying.

MOLTEN I

Ore melting
in the fertile womb.
With a long tempered rod and thick hide gloves
a man stirs
her countenance, pure of sediment,
free of lazy
shortcuts that would weaken
discrepancy.

MOLTEN 2

The she she is to be
slides, a massive tongue, off the ladle.
If she speaks it will be
in translation.

MOLTEN 3

Copper
or

crude ore in huge
cauldrons stoked and stirred in a shaft of light

under which a woman
can set her sight.

FOUNDRY

The fetching heat, the smell
verging on burning.

The fledgling concept
fired-up bubbling like lava
then cooled,
passive, satiated,
a *freed*
molten core.

Hot hot hot
it matters, hodgepodge symbol
transformed
from an easel, a sketchpad,
from a vellum sheet

an afterthought,
the tail end of its own idea:

she is *image of / the likes of*
a mother.

MAKING SKIN

The ceiling high as a frown
echoes
mallets pounding.

Tap tap tap, a journeyman's
light hold on a handle,
an apprentice's too-tight grip,
a master artisan's
whole body

tap tap tapping

a psoriasis elbow, calloused heel,
du jour classical chin uplifted.

Not beer songs but Bizet or Massenet
wielding *tap tap tap*

wielding *tap*.

Her hollow girth draped in
2-mm-thick perfection.
Stola over breasts, belly, thighs.
A diadem the same copper skin and a torch,
tablet, sandal, broken chain.

Tap the metal—

body and accoutrements reverberate
the same.

DISMANTLED

Workers break their lives
into distinctions,
unbolt wrong and right, make incomplete
the complete.

Counterclockwise, counterintuitive
undoing what they'd done.
The product:

boxed second chances
inventoried in a handwriting
men on a New York island
can't read.

STOW

Visible into invisible
the whole of her disappears
into crates.

Her brief past wrenched into pieces.
Her breath unspooled in long
mid-May days.

Hauled to the hold
she's stowed.
Labels, lists, a new man in charge.
Tied and hooked, crank-
lifted crates
swing off the dock,
the *Isère* tugs its mooring.

Two hundred boxes
one by one
pushed pulled piled maneuvered.
For three weeks, 65 men
day and night pack the hold
the hold
while Bartholdi writes down
what's where.

A WOMAN IN PIECES CROSSED A SEA

Lapping Bedloe's shore, ripples,
and seagrass swatting waves.
But this story is not about water

though a woman in pieces
crossed a sea
precariously, storm-tossed
masts, lost ballast.

Like the ocean
we change in our sleep.
Newborn tucked in a wood-slat crib
overnight
two rosette breasts.

SHE CROSSES BORDERS

On open-shackle feet
she crosses long dotted lines.
Crosses sketch to object,
ore to molten steel.
Hot to cold.
Small medium beyond large to huge.
Norway / France / New York.
Land / sea / land.
Piece, whole,
whole again to piece.
Ideal to real.
Then to now. Full to hollow.
Mother to metal.
Flesh to hammered skin.
Adamant to a five-inch sway in wind.

With a passport stamped *change*
and *be the same*,
a photo ID glib as a poster on a sheriff's wall
and signed, sealed documents
she crosses.
Fine, you say, fine. But then
who is she?

Bedloe's Island

THE YEAR BEGINS

Mid-air when the first box on a rope
swings

from the sea-battered *Isère*
to the dock.

BEFORE IS

Packed in boxes
metal against rough-cut wood or
what constitutes
buffer:
wool batting, wadded rags, a prior

incarnation of styrofoam peanuts and balls.
Cozy.
Safe from the smallest
jiggle, jolt
premonition—the box
swinging from the iron hook,
a precarious crane—
All this

is before.
The woman is before.
Disassembly, unassembly
is before.
Methodical. No entanglements.
No metaphors in knots.

WAITING

On the island the men talk.

Talk weather, talk money, talk wars,
they *talk*.

Crated time:
a year, split-seconds pass

quick as an eyelid blinking off a gnat,
slow as a palm over velvet.

Words and words
disassemble / reassemble.

Why a *torch* or *tablet* to begin with
but that meaning

will grow in it, someone meant it to mean
and *instilled*

so it does
and they ask, in the *talk talk talk*

will it last.

WINTER

The island takes root
in the stomach of a belching sea.
Roots like a pit, its fruit
bitten by brine.

Spent Rough Hawkweed
yellows under plush white snow.

You wouldn't know liberty
winters here
from looking, from turning your head—
except *hey*—
it's a woman in parts.

YEAR PAUSE SLEEP

Between bed and rising

who sleeps while the promise sleeps,
who stays awake.

Who labors day and night
while metal shapes of concocted connections
lie unstirred.

Maybe change is the shady character
fidgeting in your dream.

Maybe change is a crumbling city's
earsplitting hourly bells—either way

it's a word
with the narrowest circumference.

PAST AND FUTURE COLLIDE

Despite
long dismantled nights and days that look like night,
despite dream and pretense

no end
and no foreseeable beginning.
Despite un-
and not-knowing

her copper skin grows green.
Freckles
mapped in pre-birth from before
before.

WHY NOT BE OPTIMISTIC

Why not be optimistic,
hugely romantic, a dream afterall.
A possibility
crammed in "this side up"
"right leg ankle thigh."
Instructions: face the face south
shoulders east-west.
Unwrap, point the seven
spikes in the crown.
Rivet the broken shackles open.

Why not be optimistic.
Know-it-all illusion, wealth of light.

The ore raw, free of cynicism
pure of heart.

UNPACKING

The rookie laborer jaunts
over the island's crop of rocks—
today they start unpacking.
Veins and cartilage
and overdue fantasies of completion.
All the air, contained or loose,
splits anxiety into anticipation.
Like giving birth
but with a step-by-step paginated
manual.

THE DAY

The first nail is clawed from the crate.
The foreman in charge
pockets that nail, liberty's release,
liberty in the remaking.
Workers have been
living on Bedloe's for months
with jokes, jibes, rejoinders.
River-island humor.
Comradery isn't enough.

INVENTORY

A man pulls out lists to match lists,
checks off that one,
this, assumes
inside the nailed-shut wood slat crate

a nose.
What temptation
to pry the lid, rustle through the packing

slide a stealth hand up a nostril,
pluck a splinter hair.

AFTER WORK

Two play cassino.
One sketches a face with a mirror
and a charcoal stick.
One will read into the night
until his book topples
and the pages fan fast as waves.
One jogs the periphery when the moon is lax.
One rewrites a poem.
One plays violin.
One, in silence, cries.
They eat in their makeshift mess
and winter in chilblain.
Days fold in an accordion end to end.
Men pile tossed planks for firewood,
pile bent nails,
draw diagrams in dirt to try to grasp
the master's plan.

UNPACKING I

She is laid out in pieces.
One foot on a diadem spike.
One wrist

on the lettered tablet. Broken ankle shackle,
one chain link under her neck.
Brows and chin

cleft to cleft.
Five cramped fingers. Not alive yet

form/body.

UNPACKING 2

The tip of the nail pops from the wood
or slips
from the wood
and under the lid a green-speckled
foot.
Corrosion
that protects from corrosion.
The heel a hue of moss
and mildew.

ALL PARTS ACCOUNTED FOR

All parts unpacked
accounted for we think (labels scribbled
and in French).

Nez, naso, nase, nariz
nostrils full of dust, pollen, hindsight.
If the angle of her nasal canal
were less acute
she would not attract every Brooklyn and Hoboken
smokestack's detritus.

THE MEN WAKE THE WOMAN

The men wake the woman
from spellbound, pitch-dark limbo.

Curves their leather gloves lift
arrange, affix.
Graft metal skin to metal bone.

Complicated 3-D puzzles, scrambled clues,
odd metaphors

foreign instructions,
down-home familiar tools.

HERE

She is

physically or not
a single idea or pile of many pieces

here, already here

the hole of her invisibility
to be filled by her return.

Midway between Jersey's riveredge
and Brooklyn Bridge filigree spires

between soft decaying buffer
and hard new air

her impertinence
is engaging.

THE RISK

Pause, a year of

not knowing
if a rivet will reunite
two and two.

Pounding sun and salted wind,
look, a cardinal

simple and red.

She waits to begin
seriously

and vertical.

ARMATURE BONES AS WE HAVE THEM

Bones as we have them
wide steel ribs

ulnae and radii, 1,830 branched hyperboles,
femurs, tibia

grow from the concrete foundation.
Copper saddles

straddle the iron bars, rivet the skin in place,
skin

the primary structure.

SHACKLES

Not everyone's ankles could snap open these shackles,
with the force of an edict
pull them apart.

Chains chains chains grew as she grew, larger.
Steel and steel harder.

Links so massive
yet from their charcoal sketch inception, light
and colossally broken.

She snapped them
in Colmar before leaving and packed them
and now their warning
she wears

as if the effort was yesterday's with no time
to clean up the mess.

Isn't that where symbol begins—
in remains of fragmentation.

HOLLOW HEAD

Hoisted last her hollow head
swings.

Brooklyn shipyards catch in her eye.
Tankers, tugs.
Fog slaps her cheek—
Complete!

The bolted-tight copper
concept nests in the hole of her neck

airtight.

SKIN OVER AIR

Skin that covers her
is jungled islands and rocky archipelagos
patched together
seamlessly.
Blotched tundra, taupe sandbars
iridescent reefs.
Her skin hangs
loose like hand-me-down trousers,
like scruffled skirts of pompous linen.
Flesh and cloth pimpled
so green the speckles
blend into one
continuous acne shroud.
Hers is unlikely skin
measured, cut, and snapped into place.
Rivets in her shoulders,
rivets in her face.

EVERYONE'S IN THE ACT

Little pork Lady Libertys in the butchershop window

Deep-brown sculpted bittersweet in the chocolatier's

A diadem crowns a carved pumpkin face

The dressmaker's stola-draped mannequin

Everybody celebrates: in cotton balls, in blocks of soap

In all material but fish heads, asphaltum, or gauze

She's an imported cousin or long-lost aunt

Sister if you look hard

Where to seat her at the table?

Do you invite her at all? They say

She's raucous when silent, silent when asked to speak

NEW GAL ON THE BLOCK I

Air is her core, her blood
how she

stays awake.

Air is her skeletal secret and muscles that keep her erect.

Air is / she is
her liberty all that that means and she is

built into, standing in
air / air holds her / I hold her / you

we, our air, our air holds her

up.

Exposed. Shivering in rain.
The fire of a million
eyes watching and she is shivering in rain.

Bolts girdle doubt and doubletake.

A U.S. girl now: debutante.
Fluffed-up goosedown pillows.
Pink diary beside the bed.

A U.S. girl now: shuttles, cocks, bobbin cones.
Cast-iron sweltering kitchens.
Steaming presses.
On her knees all night scrubbing.

AS IF QUEEN OF THE RIGHT THING

She issues orders: *look at me,*
look—

Can't miss the monarch in the harbor,
cartoon dialog balloon at her lips.
The scripts that matter
are stuck in her hollow head.

Corrosion that protects from corrosion
softens her stark silhouette.
Have you sympathy?
She's royalty lost in foreign water
covered in hives.

PROMISED

We were promised her eyes
not blinded by starlight
will stare down gobbledegook, glare
at hodgepodge interpretation.
We were promised critique.
Don't misunderstand,
she is in no way a nodding bobble-head—
but who fed us promises?
Predicting what results, recorded where?
The tablet is monosyllabic.
The crown, seven points askew.
If she sees the pile of props behind the curtain
she's not telling.
Her lips have been carved closed.

FROM A DISTANCE

A complicated host of shape and form.
The horizontal slightly vertical
upper arm plugs into an elliptical sleeve
and the square tablet at the bent wrist
hunkers in thick tube fingers.
Stiff fabric drapes in folds.
A coif tidy as combed
hills of a not-yet-seeded wheatfield
nests under the rectangular
windows in the crown of spikes
pointing to seven distances.
An empire-size ring
encircles the waffle-cone torch,
the vanilla flame melting.

It all appears to fit.
What you see is what you get.
But note the lack of *negative* space,
those odd leftover shapes
between subject and ground.

NEW GAL ON THE BLOCK 3

If you know her you know her well.
Her jabs at the sky no surprise

and when her raised arm sways
you don't question
her strength. The torch
as if balsa, her hand
a modelmaker's gentle vise.

You say, look down—
the pylon pier is rocking, we not she
are swaying.

Don't belittle her, you say,
we should be that sure-footed.

ON THE ISLAND SHE IS BORN

She is born with broken

shackles on her feet
broken—
but shackles.

Born dragging her symbol self up the pedestal stair,
iron rings clawing her ankles
like fingernails of a clinging child
begging.

Concept is that child
clinging, begging to be lifted and held.
Begging for a story at bedtime
it's all right, tomorrow
is another day.
Lifted to her mother's shoulder's
unencumbered view
and coddled
as she outgrows spasm by spasm
her birth.

Concept is her pocked face
scarred and blemished.
Her eyes don't blink, her eyes stare
despite the bright light
her lids are flaccid but her eyes
don't blink.

She is born from concept, pregnant possibility.
Born from herself in a contrived
circular way that coils
reason into contradiction.

Aghast and hardened she is born
full form.

FACT IS

Despite hoopla, she remains
unbejeweled

her neck simply cast, unweighted.
Her wrists unadorned.

Fact is

her flat eyes
gaze in only one direction.

If on this island she is symbol, then all of it—
the southeast she faces

the thick French plaits covering her ears.
Fact is fact.

She's vertical
in a horizontal harbor

topped
with a diadem of spikes.

THE DIADEM SPIKES POINT TO CELEBRATION

Her straight-ahead gaze blocks your peripheral vision

The city is eclipsed behind

Bands of blind beggars, we lean into any stranger's arm

Spiked headdress, a goddess, *bow down*

Confetti disperses the sunlight, fireworks shatter the dark

Speeches, battalions, wheeled cannons

One, two, skip a few, ninety-nine, a hundred

THE DIADEM SPIKES POINT TO THE HORIZON

Eight months before she opens her copper blind eyes

Slim fifty miles south, fewer when Jim Crow flies

Mingo Jack, short, stout

Dragged from his cell, blood on the loop-rope knot

Authorities say no prints, the *Times* writes,

New Jersey tries to prove

The mob lynched "the wrong Negro"

THE DIADEM SPIKES POINT TO LABOR

The ten year old is *out there working*, out there

A woman's hand lunges for the penny piecework

Through the spinning gears

Day, night, and sweat behind grime-painted windows

Doors locked, menstrual flow puddles on the bench

Tens of thousands spill into Broadway, first of May, Union Square

The last to protest is not the last

The bakers union banner: hours, ages, wages—*rise up!*

THE DIADEM SPIKES POINT TO PERMISSIONS GRANTED

Five hundred Chiricahuas torn from their land

Cattle-driven and whipped

Cornered and scalped. Slayed and scalped

Train windows nailed shut. Shit, piss, and vomit

Like animals, like nonhumans

Nonhumans, not even a species

Prisoners of war for twenty-seven years

THE DIADEM SPIKES POINT TO PERMISSIONS
NOT GRANTED

In a land where not a single woman has liberty

Suffragists steer a small rented boat to the front of the flotilla

Banners unfurl *a litany of unjust laws*

Not a one-line curio in the *New York Times*

Stola, shackle, broken chain—make of it what you want

Copper, symbol, air

Just that

WHAT IF SHE WANTS TO CHANGE

What if she wants to loop her arms in silver,
neck in ruby and onyx.

Slouch, droop, drop her chin,
ease her roiling gut, say what she thinks
say what she sees, say
the uninscribed

unscripted.

What if she wants to disobey,
tell the sister you turned away, *I hear*

helplessly I hear

and lug her half-shackled feet
off the pedestal,
slip from the sandal one toe, two—
kick the illusion apart.

What if she wants to strip naked.
In a far hemisphere. On a desert dune.
No one will find her, need her,
thrust their palms out, take take take.
She'd escape
the ankle-iron however-broken chains.
Sever her feet if she has to—
stand on feetless limbs,
the first step.